Flame – The Animal Saver

Flame and the Mouse

Anna-Stina Johansson

This book is dedicated to the wonderful mice and all the other amazing small creatures. May it come a day when all people show these beautiful creatures respect and compassion.

Flame – The Animal Saver

Flame and the Mouse

Late one evening I couldn't sleep. I got up, looked out and admired the big, white, beautiful full moon through the window. The thermometer showed -30 degrees! Brr, how cold! Lucky me, since I'm almost never cold, I smiled to myself. It's definitely worse for animals. Then I spotted something small and dark on the snow outside my house. I hurried out, and when I got there I saw that it was a little wood mouse.

He was unconscious, and he was barely breathing. I put my right hand on him.

"Wake up! Wake up! Wake up!"

The mouse was brought back to life again and smiled.

"Thanks, you have saved my life!"

I smiled back. "Don't worry! I save animals! That's the way I am!"

I picked up the little fellow in my arms and asked how come that he had got unconscious. Then the wood mouse told me that he had lived near a stable. The people there didn't like mice, so they put out rat poison. His whole family and all of his friends had died. He was the only survivor, and that made him so sad so he went straight out into the forest with just one thing on his mind, and that was to get as far away from people as possible. Finally, the mouse ended up outside my house.

It was a long time since he had eaten. The cold and the exhaustion had made him unconscious. What a poor little guy I thought.

I told him about Borderland and asked if he wanted me to bring him there. His tiny face lit up when he heard that!

I carried him to a few spruces that were standing close together and put him down there.

"Here it's a little bit warmer. Stay here, while I go and get some food for you."

When I got back into the house, I took out a backpack and put a blanket in it. Then I took out a little piece of fruit and a big slice of juicy bread. I brought all the things with me and went out to my little friend. He ate the fruit right away and then some of the bread.

Then I tucked him in, in the blanket which was in the backpack. Next to him I put what was left of the bread, so that he could eat whenever he felt hungry. Of course, I let the flap of the backpack stay open so that he could see where we were going. I put on the backpack, and then we started rambling towards Borderland.

It was a splendid night. The moon lit up the dark landscape. All the hills and the valleys looked soft in the moonlight. The stars were shining brightly on the velvet sky. The wood mouse wondered if I could teach him some constellations and so I did. I told him that the constellation that looks like a big wagon is called Big Dipper or Great Bear, and the one that looks like a small wagon is called Little Dipper or Little Bear.

The sign which looks like a "W" is called Cassiopeia. While I taught my friend the names of the stars and star signs, we saw the northern lights.

We stopped for a while and looked at this amazing natural phenomenon. It was of different colors; green, white and purple. It was moving back and forth in different directions all over the sky. It was one of the most beautiful northern lights that both the mouse and I had ever seen. When the northern lights began to disappear, we started walking again.

When we got to Borderland, I took off my backpack and put the mouse down on the soft grass. I assured him that he was safe from all people here. He strolled away to mingle with the other rodents. Then he came back to me and thanked me once again for taking him there. I told him that the pleasure was all mine. His joy was shining from his peppercorn-colored eyes when he looked at me. Then he started playing with his new friends.

www.ingramcontent.com/pod-product-compliance
Lightning Source LLC
Chambersburg PA
CBHW041810040426
42449CB00001B/49